# The Way of
# Our People

# The Way of Our People

## Arnold A. Griese

*For Trapper Your Mom thought you would enjoy this book. Dogs do play an important part in the story*

*[signature]*

*Oct 1999*

Boyds Mills Press

Copyright © 1975 by Arnold A. Griese
All rights reserved

Published by Caroline House
Boyds Mills Press, Inc.
A Highlights Company
815 Church Street
Honesdale, Pennsylvania 18431
Printed in the United States of America

Originally published by Thomas Y. Crowell Company, New York, 1977.
First Boyds Mills Press paperback edition, 1997.

Library of Congress Cataloging in Publication Data

Griese, Arnold A.   The way of our people.
Summary: In 1838 in the village of Anvik a young Athabaskan boy, unable to overcome
his fear of hunting alone, finds other ways of helping his village.
[1. Alaska—Fiction. 2. Indians of North America—Fiction]
I. Title.   PZ7.G8812Way [Fic] 74-23086
ISBN 1-56397-648-X

The text of this book is set in Garamond Book.
Book designed by Amy O'Hare

10 9 8 7 6 5 4 3 2 1

*For a special baby, Charity Hope, who will always be remembered.*

*For my granddaughters, Tacha, Helen, and Molly.*

*And for my newest great-granddaughter, Miranda Jane.*

# CONTENTS

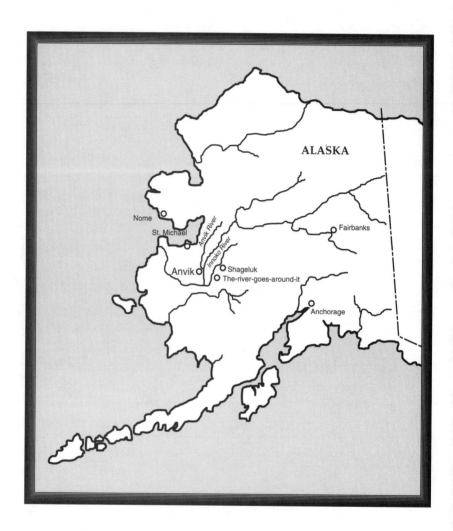

# ABOUT THIS STORY

This story tells about an Athabaskan Indian village in Alaska a long time ago. It tries to tell what it was like then to be an Athabaskan boy, or an Athabaskan girl, living in the village called Anvik. What it was like to be afraid to do the things you had to do to be an Athabaskan.

Today there is still a village called Anvik at the place where the Anvik River runs into the Yukon River, and Athabaskan Indians still live there. They still love their rivers, hills, and forests because it is the way of their people.

# 1

# Feast of the First Hunt

Long ago, in the year 1838, in the village called Anvik, an Athabaskan Indian boy stood waiting outside the door of the Kashim—a meeting place used by his people at important times. Now was such an important time. The outside door of the Kashim was made from the skin of the bear and through it the boy, Kano, could hear the beating of drums and people clapping and singing. All of this was to honor him.

Kano shivered as he stood alone and waited. He shivered because it was night and the night was cold. It was spring, but snow still lay thick on the ground; ice still covered the Anvik River in front of the Kashim and shut out the sound of its fast-moving waters. Just over the hill, in back of the Kashim, a full moon touched the very tips of the tall spruce trees. By its light Kano could see smoke coming from the smoke hole of his own house.

Over the sounds coming from inside the Kashim, Kano could hear the north wind blowing hard down another river, the great Yukon, which lay just on the other side of the hill. It whistled through the spruce trees on top of that hill, but here, where Kano stood waiting, the air was cold and still.

Hundreds of years before Kano was born his people had picked this spot and had built their village here. They had picked this spot because there were many fish where the two rivers came together, because there were many animals in the forest nearby, and because the hill and the trees kept out the cold north wind.

Now the waiting was over. Women came up out of the doorway of Kano's house. They carried big wooden bowls of cooked moose meat—meat from a moose Kano himself had killed. As the women came up the path to the Kashim, Kano stepped away from the door to let them pass. His older sister, Maya, led the way. She did not speak or look his way as she went by, nor did the other women.

Kano followed the last woman down the steps. The smell of cooked moose meat filled his nose and made his mouth water, even though he was thinking of other things.

Then, as if by magic, all noise stopped as Kano stepped through the last doorway into the Kashim itself. Without a sound the dancers took their seats. Women who carried the bowls of meat set them down in front of the loved-fire in the middle of the room and then sat down too.

Kano stood looking into the loved-fire, his flashing dark eyes matching his shiny black hair. Soon he would be old enough to live in the Kashim and then he too could help take care of this important fire. Every day it gave off heat for the sweat baths. Every day it warmed the big Kashim while the younger men sat around and made things needed by the people of the village. And during the long, cold winter nights the old men lay by this fire and told stories until all were asleep.

As Kano waited, the men sat on benches all around the sides of the Kashim, all with their eyes on him. The only women in the room were those who carried in the bowls of cooked meat. They sat on the floor with their heads down.

At last one man in this big room rose to his feet. This was Kano's father. He stood straight, and tall, and proud—a hunter whom all the people of this village looked up to. Much would be expected of the son of such a father, Kano thought as he walked to stand beside this man.

All was quiet. The light from the big clay lamps in the middle of the room flickered and smoked a little, and all waited. Then Kano's father spoke, "This is my son. He has already seen thirteen summers. More than six or seven summers ago he killed his first animal, a rabbit, but I waited for this time to have his Feast of the First Hunt. The meat you see by the fire, and which you will soon eat, comes from the moose my son has killed. Three days ago he went with his dogs far up on our Anvik River."

As his father talked, Kano saw Napak. He did not like Napak and Napak did not like him. They were always trying to beat each other in games and in hunting. Napak was older; he was fifteen. Kano knew he had shamed Napak by killing a moose first. But Kano was worried. Some day Napak might find out Kano's secret; if he did, that would bring shame not just on Kano but on his father too.

How much longer could he hide this terrible secret? Kano kept thinking about this as his father said, "I went with him only to help find the moose and to help clean and skin it. He hit it first five times with his arrows. But this was a big moose and the arrows only stopped him. Then when the moose turned to fight, Kano killed him with his knife that he had tied to a pole. I stood ready to help but he did not need it."

Kano's father stopped talking and both of them stepped up to the place of honor and sat down on a thick beaverskin blanket.

Quiet talk filled the big room but Kano saw that Napak did not talk. Napak sat with his head down.

Soon the sound of a drum stopped the talking, and at the same time, four dancers came and began dancing in front of the place of honor. Kano's eyes saw and his ears heard, but his mind was on other things. What would he do when he would have to go on a hunt alone? Almost as if to answer that question, the dance stopped and an old man spoke, "This boy, Kano, son of a great hunter, has been taught well. He has shown himself to be brave. He is now ready to go alone to hunt and to bring much meat to this village."

The old man sat down. Once more Kano's father stood up and spoke, "Since this boy's mother is dead, his sister and those with her will bring the meat. But before they do, I will take the first piece to the one called 'Killer-of-bears.' He is now old but was once the greatest hunter in our village."

Kano watched as his father walked over to where the women sat. One of them put meat in a small bowl and gave it to him. Kano's father then crossed over to the front of the Kashim where the old men sat. As he set the bowl down in front of Killer-of-bears he said, "May your animal song bring luck to my son when the time comes in which the fish do not run in our two rivers and the animals hide in their homes under the ground in the hills."

Killer-of-bears smiled as he looked up at Kano's father. He then began eating. The women saw this and began bringing meat to the others.

Kano and his father then left the place of honor, but waited until all the other men were eating before taking anything themselves. His sister, Maya, brought a bowl to Kano. She smiled at him as she whispered, "I have saved that big piece on top for you, my important brother."

Her smile, and the way she spoke, told Kano she wanted him not to be sad. He took the big piece and smiled back at her as she moved on. Maya knew he should be happy tonight. She knew how to make him smile and forget.

Most of the men had finished eating and the women were picking up the empty bowls when Napak came over to where Kano stood. He did not speak and Kano could think of nothing to say. At last Kano asked, "Did you like the meat?"

Napak did not smile as he answered, "It is like any other moose meat. Why should it taste better just because you killed it?" He turned to walk away, then added, "Maybe if I had a father who would always take me with him when he went hunting and who would help me find the moose, maybe then I would have killed my first moose before you did."

Kano did not try to answer. It was true, Napak's father had been dead many years now and in Napak's family there were three children besides himself, all younger than Napak. Napak's mother had few furs and little time to sew. But Maya always made new clothes for Kano; even now he was wearing a new muskrat parka she had made just for this feast.

Kano knew it was wrong to be angry at Napak for what he said, but still he was angry. And he was also afraid; afraid that Napak would find out his secret. If Napak did, he would not keep it to himself. The whole village would then know he, Kano, was not a brave hunter.

Kano moved around the Kashim. Men sat talking about the white men called Russians who were now coming to trade with the Athabaskans and the Eskimo. Some told stories while still others worked on muskrat stretchers and other things, and watched. Men looked at Kano without speaking as he passed by, but their eyes told him they were glad that he would be a great hunter like his father. Their village called Anvik needed good hunters.

Their trust in him, that he would become a great hunter, made him feel even worse than Napak's words. He needed to tell his secret to someone.

Without waiting any longer, and without letting his father know, he slipped out. He must talk to Maya.

The moon was now high in the sky, but Kano could still hear the wind whistling through the trees on the hill above him. As he walked down the path he could see that Maya had already put the cover back over the smoke hole on the top of their house. Good, he thought, the women will be gone and Grandmother will be asleep.

Kano climbed carefully down into the dark hallway and saw light around the bottom of the skin, which was the door leading into the house. Bending over and stepping inside he noticed that his grandmother's side of the house was dark; she was asleep. On the other side he saw Maya sitting on a bench bed. She was trying to thread a needle by the light of a small lamp sitting on the ledge in back of her.

Kano sat down next to her and watched. Maya finished threading the needle and looked up. "It pleased Father to give this feast in your honor; then why did you not show him your happiness? A good son should not act as you did when he is being honored."

Maya was four years older than Kano, and because she cooked his food and made his clothes she sometimes scolded him like a mother. This Kano did not always like.

Maya saw she had hurt him and went on, "I am sorry. Something is very wrong for you to be so worried on this night of the feast."

"Maya, I must tell you something. You will be ashamed to have me as a brother after I tell you, but I must."

Maya put her sewing to one side. "Do not be afraid to tell me."

Kano's eyes were filled with tears as he stammered, "Father and . . . and the men of our village think I am brave. It is not so. I am not brave; I am afraid!"

Maya waited for him to say more, but Kano sat with his head down trying to keep her from seeing his tears. Then she said, "Tonight Father told the men you killed a moose all by yourself. Father does not lie. I think you are very brave."

Kano's head was still down but his tears had stopped. "Yes, when Father is with me I am brave. I am not afraid of the animals. All the animals in the forest are friends of our people. They let us catch them in our traps and let us hunt them so that we can live. No, I am not afraid, even of the bear."

"Then what do you fear?"

Kano now looked into her face as he answered, "I do not know. It is something I cannot see."

Maya said, "It is a spirit of the forest then, a Nakani. All hunters fear the Nakani when they are in the forest, even your father. You will learn to live with this fear. You are still young; you will learn this."

"But I have tried and I can't. Remember when I was very little and my father took me out and showed me how to set snares for rabbits and grouse? I never went by myself to check them. I always found some way to get you or my mother to go with me. And when I was older, I looked carefully for good places near the village to set the snares. And even then I would always take one of my dogs with me and run all the way."

Maya said, "But that was long ago. Have you never been in the forest by yourself since then?"

Kano answered, "No, not far from the village. In the summer we are always together at the fish camp, and I was always with my father when we hunted because he was teaching me. But now it is different. This fall I will have to go far up the Anvik River to hunt caribou, and I must go alone. I will not be able to do it; this will bring shame to all my family."

"How do you know you will not be able to go by yourself? Have you tried?"

Kano answered, "Yes, I have tried. Just last fall Father took me with him to hunt. When we were near the caribou, he told me to stay in one place to watch for them while he went to hunt farther on. As soon as he left I became afraid. Something seemed to be watching me, but when I looked there was nothing. I thought of running after Father, but he left no trail." Kano stopped as if hoping that Maya would say something.

Maya said, "Yes, I have heard Father say this is the way it is when the Nakani is near."

Kano went on, "It did not go away and I was even more afraid. I tried hard not to call out for my father. Then something happened. It was as if my brain went empty. I must have run, but I do not remember anything until I found myself on a trail we had used before. I followed it to camp. My bow and arrows were gone. I did not know where they were and I was too afraid to look for them." Kano stopped again and Maya went quickly to put oil in the lamp.

When she had finished she sat down and asked, "And what did you do then?"

Kano answered, "I lay down on the grass and pulled a beaverskin blanket over me so that nothing could see me. I was still afraid and wanted to cry, but if I did something would hear me. I tried to lie very still but I could not keep from shaking. At last I must have gone to sleep. Father came before dark and found me sleeping."

Maya stopped him to ask, "And did you tell him what happened?"

Kano looked away as he answered, "I was too filled with shame. I told him I had seen a bear and had run away leaving my bow and arrows behind."

"Do you think he believed you?" Maya asked.

"I do not know. He did not ask about the bear. The next morning we went and found my bow and arrows near where he had told me to stay. Then he kept me with him until he killed a caribou."

They both sat without talking. The light flickered low, and Maya turned to push the moss wick further down into the oil. At last she asked, "Would it help if you have your two dogs with you on the hunt this fall?"

Kano thought for a while before answering, "Father and I will take them as far as our camp in the hills but there we must leave them, and there is where I must go by myself to hunt." He stopped, but before Maya could speak he went on, "And what will I do in these next days when we go with Napak's family to make a spring camp on the lake? Napak must not find out about my fear."

"Do not worry. I will not tell anyone what you have told me."

"That is true," Kano said. "But at camp you know there is always a chance that I will be expected to go out by myself."

"Yes," Maya answered, "but maybe I will find a way to keep this from happening." Then she added, "Now we must go to bed. Father will not sleep in the Kashim tonight, and tomorrow there will be much work getting ready to go to spring camp."

Kano stood and smiled down at Maya. "You know my secret and are not ashamed of me."

# 2

# Spring Camp

Kano's father had never taken his family to spring camp before. Always before, when the days grew warmer but when snow still covered the ground, he and other men would take sleds to a small Eskimo village by the great waters. White men had now built their own village near there called St. Michael. The men from Kano's village took wooden bowls and skins and traded these for seal oil and other things the Eskimo or white men might have. But this year Kano's father did not go. He wanted Kano to learn about spring camp.

And there was much for Kano to learn. The morning after the feast the family was busy making ready for the move to a lake not far from the village. Because Napak's family did not have a father, Kano's father invited that family to go with them.

The men's job was to get the big traveling canoe and

the smaller hunting canoes ready. The warm sun made Kano take off his parka as he worked with Napak getting the canoes down from the racks in front of the houses. After the long winter it felt good to be out in the sun. Soon they would be camping by the lake and spending the long spring days tending the fish traps and hunting muskrats. Kano smiled at Napak and Napak smiled back. The anger of last night was forgotten.

Maya called for them to come and help get the food out of the underground cache. Kano's father let them go, and they both ran over to help.

Maya and Napak's mother were happy too—happy to be getting away from their dark winter houses and to be getting fresh fish to cook for their families. The two women were laughing as they argued over what food and clothing to take and what pots and bowls they would need. Kano's father had said they could take only that which would go on one sled, and there were so many things they wanted to take.

Napak's younger brother and two sisters were excited, too. They showed it by laughing, talking, and getting in the way of those working. Even Kano's grandmother, the one who was called "Basket-maker," was excited about going. She was very old, but she helped by carefully packing away everything that was set aside to be taken, and she smiled as she worked.

After dark, when the crust of the snow was again frozen, the men made the first trip, taking the canoes and some of the tools needed to build the fish traps.

Even though Kano and his father had dogs to pull the sleds, Kano and Napak had to help by pushing while Kano's father made sure the birch bark on the canoes would not be broken when the sleds passed by trees and bushes.

By midnight they were back and ready to make the last trip. Friends who were not going stood waiting to say good-bye while Grandmother and Napak's younger brother and two sisters were loaded onto one of the sleds. Kano and the others would walk or help push the sleds. Kano was tired and sleepy, but he would not let others see this.

Someone who was staying called out, "Do not go on bad ice." Someone else called out another warning. All of this to show that those leaving for spring camp would be missed by those staying behind.

This last trip to the lake went faster. Everyone was in a hurry to get there and everyone helped the dogs by taking turns pushing. And Kano's father did not have to worry about the canoes.

When they came to the lake, Grandmother and the children were already sleeping and were left in the sled. Everyone else slept the few hours until morning with their clothes on, lying on spruce branches that had been cut earlier, and each covered with a beaverskin blanket. Kano and his father were the last to lie down. They had to first unhitch and tie the dogs. Kano took one last look around before sinking down into the spruce branches and covering himself with the beaverskin blanket. The moon was gone, the night was dark, no fire burned, but he felt safe here with other people close by.

Early the next morning Kano's father started a fire. He and the two boys started cutting poles needed for the frame of their spruce-branch house while the women cooked enough food to last all day.

By evening the house was finished. Kano thought it looked like a big arrowhead pointing straight into the sky. Spruce branches covered its sides from the ground right up to the very tip.

The next few days were warm, and bright, and filled with sunshine. Fish traps were built and put into the lake, but there was also time for Kano and Napak to take the hunting canoes and go along the edges of the lake looking for muskrat houses. Ice still covered the middle of the lake.

The first time out they came back toward evening without seeing any signs of muskrats, but Kano had shot two ducks with the spear thrower and darts his father had made for him. Napak had no spear thrower and Kano saw that he felt ashamed, being older than Kano and coming back without any fresh meat for his family. Kano offered to show him how to use his spear thrower and to let him try it out the next day, but Napak walked away saying he must help his mother.

The first week at camp passed quickly, and Kano stopped worrying about having to go out into the forest alone.

Everyone had work to do there at the lake. Kano's father took the fish from the trap and put them up on racks to dry after Maya and Napak's mother had cleaned them. Kano and Napak had found muskrat houses and often would take Maya with them. She was good at making the sucking sound that brought the muskrats out of their houses and gave Kano and Napak a chance to shoot them with their bows and arrows. Kano was happy.

But all this changed the evening Napak came toward camp paddling very hard. As he reached the shore he jumped from the canoe and came running and shouting, "A moose. I saw a big moose on the hill in back of the camp."

Kano's father listened as Napak told more about where he had seen the moose. Kano looked over at Maya. Her eyes told him that she too knew what would happen now.

As soon as Napak stopped talking Maya said, "But, Father, with the fish running in the traps and the muskrats just right for making parkas, you and the boys cannot take time to chase after a moose."

When Kano's father did not speak, Napak answered, "But the moose will give us much meat and the skin will be used too."

Kano saw that Maya was trying to help him. She spoke again to her father, "Father, you know how hard it would be to kill a moose now when the snow is almost gone and he can run fast, and now when the air brings quickly the smell of man to his nose. Remember, just a few weeks back you and Kano trailed the moose for many days before Kano could get close enough to kill it. And then the snow was still deep and the moose could not run fast."

Kano's father still said nothing and Napak now turned to Kano, "Have you nothing to say? Do you not wish to hunt? Will you let your sister tell the men of this camp that they cannot hunt the moose when they have already seen it?"

Kano said nothing and now his father answered Napak, "Among our people the women do not tell the men how and when to hunt. But my daughter is right: this is not the time to hunt moose."

These words took away Kano's fear. But then his father went on, "We can do nothing now in the darkness, but tomorrow morning, before the sun is in the sky, Kano, Napak, and I shall take our bows and arrows and each of us shall go a different way until we meet on top of the hill. If one of us finds the moose, he will give the owl sound. If no one finds the moose before we meet, it means he is already far away down the other side of the hill, and we will come back to camp."

Kano's father had decided; both Kano and Maya knew no more should be said. Kano would have to go or let Napak find out he was afraid to go into the forest alone.

The evening food was eaten without talk; even the children sat quietly. After eating, Kano's father said, "Tonight everyone to bed early. There must be no sound. The moose might come close to camp. And morning will come only too soon."

As Kano came from feeding the dogs, Maya stood outside the house waiting. She whispered, "Tomorrow morning, while Napak's mother and the children are still sleeping, I will slip out and go with you."

Kano whispered back, "You must not. Napak's mother will wake and find you gone. Then Napak will find out."

"Don't worry, I will think of something. Remember, tomorrow as you walk in the wood, you will not see me, but you will not be alone." And before Kano could say more, she moved quickly into the house to the side where the women and children slept.

The night was long for Kano. He was already sitting up when his father turned over to wake him. The three moved out of the house quietly. Napak was to go straight up the middle of the hill to the top, Kano around to the right, and Kano's father around to the left.

Kano walked quickly to where the trees began and looked back. He could not see Maya, but he knew she would follow. He would not be alone. But what would happen afterward? Perhaps, if they got the moose, Napak's mother would be so busy cutting and drying the meat that she would forget to ask why Maya was away from camp.

But they did not get the moose. They did not find the moose even though Kano hunted as his father had taught him. He walked quietly for a while, then he stopped to look and to listen. Kano did this over and over again until he came to the top of the hill. Napak was already there, sitting and waiting. Both sat and listened, hoping to hear Kano's father make the sound of the owl.

But no sound came. At last Kano looked up and saw his father moving toward them like a shadow. Not a sound did he make.

All three were unhappy as they walked down the hill. They had to go back without the moose that would have fed many mouths.

The three came back to camp before the morning was over. Kano looked for Maya and saw her cutting up fish near the traps. During that afternoon everyone worked hard to get all the fish cleaned and put on the racks. The boys did not go hunting muskrats that day. Kano tried to talk to Maya, but she always seemed to be near someone.

That night, after everyone had eaten and everything was cleaned up, Maya asked Kano to take her out in his hunting canoe to the muskrat houses. Kano was glad to take her.

Just then, Napak's mother said, "Maya, I still do not know why you took most of the morning to go look for more muskrat houses. You knew this morning we would have no men helping us with the fish. And you did not even take your brother's canoe. No wonder you took so long."

Maya looked at Kano, then at her father, and then she put her head down as her father spoke, "Yes, Maya, this is not like you. Why did you leave when there was so much work to be done?"

Maya stood still with her head down, and did not answer. At last her father said, "Put on your parka and come with me. Maybe there is something you should tell me."

Maya followed her father out. They were almost to the canoes before he looked back and saw that Kano was following too. He spoke softly but there was anger in his voice, "I wish to speak only to Maya."

Kano looked straight at his father as he said, "If Maya did wrong, she did it because of me. Father, I wish to speak first."

His father did not answer, but turned and walked along the shore to some rocks and there sat down. Kano and Maya stood before him. Kano spoke, "Father, it is not Maya who brings shame to you, it is I. I am afraid to go into the forest by myself. Maya knew this so she followed me this morning."

Their father looked at Maya, "Is this so?"

"Yes, Father, but Kano is still young. Like all hunters, he fears the Nakani."

Kano stopped her to say, "But when I am afraid I run like the timid rabbit. All of my life I have been afraid to be alone in the forest. I have tried not to be, but always my brain goes empty and I run."

Their father sat for a long time, looking out over the water and thinking. When at last he spoke there was anger in his face and in his voice, and Kano looked away. "Kano, you are too old to run when you are afraid. At the feast the old men of our village said you were ready to go by yourself to hunt caribou when the time-of-the-falling-leaves comes. You will go, then, and by yourself. These many years I have shown you many things you need to know to be a good hunter. I can do no more. You must now learn this one more thing you need to be a hunter among our people."

Their father now stood up and laid his hand on Kano's shoulder. His face and voice were no longer angry. "If you do not go on this hunt, you must leave our village forever."

After he said these words he walked away toward the forest to be alone. Maya touched Kano's arm as she said, "He is sad, too, but it is the way of our people."

That night it rained. The cloudy sky and the wetness only added to Kano's unhappiness. Now he worked even harder. Every day he helped keep the fires under the drying fish and every day he went to hunt muskrats and brought back at least one. At night he would skin these and put them on stretchers he himself made.

All this time he was thinking, and from all this thinking there came a plan. On the day the traveling and hunting canoes were loaded for the trip out of the lake, down to the river and home, Kano was ready to tell his plan to Maya and his father.

# 3

# One-Who-Lives-Alone

It was early morning as Kano stood watching other families making ready to leave the village for their summer camps on the Yukon River. He watched as the big traveling canoes and the smaller hunting canoes were carried to the river and loaded. Soon his family would be going too. But he would not be going with them this year, not if his father let him carry out his plan.

He turned to Maya and his father who stood nearby and said, "Father, it will not be long before the fish that now swim in the river will be drying on the racks at our summerhouse, the berries will be ripe, and the geese will again be crying to us as they fly away to another land. Much work waits for me at our summerhouse, many fish need to be caught and made ready for next winter. But that will not help me make ready for the fall hunt."

He stopped talking. A squirrel chattered in a tree near him, and his father asked, "And what is it you wish to do?"

Kano answered, "I wish to go now into the forest and live near where the Old One stays. There I will learn to live with my fear. There perhaps Old One will tell me his secret."

Maya said, "Do you not know that many of our people fear the Old One? Do you not know that some think he is himself one of the Nakani?"

Kano answered, "My father and I have passed by the little lake with its big trees where Old One lives. I have seen him sitting by his house. I am not afraid of Old One."

Now their father spoke, "Yes, you are needed at our summerhouse, but there is a greater need for you to do this other. Maya will help me, and Grandmother is strong; she will help too."

Maya asked, "When will you go?"

Kano answered, "Now. Your canoes are ready. There is nothing more I can do here. If I leave now, I will come to Old One's place before night."

It did not take long for Kano to get ready. He would carry little with him. This summer he would make his home in the forest, he would find his food there, and he would try to learn its secrets.

When at last Kano stood with his packsack on his back and his bow in hand, Maya hurried out with a skin bag full of fish eggs that she knew Kano liked. Their father found room for it on top of the pack.

It was time to go. Kano said, "Father, you and Maya will need help bringing the dried fish up the river when you come back to the village. Leave my canoe here and before the summer is over I will come to help you."

His father said only, "I will leave it for you."

Then Kano looked into Maya's eyes. They were sad as she said, "Soon our family will be together again."

Kano turned and walked away. He did not look back as he took the trail into the forest.

Late that same night Kano came through the tall spruce trees to the shore of a lake. The sun was still shining. So it was at this time of the year in the land of Kano's people. Not far away he saw smoke. Old One's place was near.

As he stood thinking of what to do next, all was still except for the soft sound of the wind moving through the spruce branches and the call of a raven sitting in a birch tree across the lake. Then out of the stillness he felt something else, as if something were watching him. It was like that other time when he waited alone for the caribou. And again fear came into his body. But this time when he looked he saw something. It was Old One standing next to a tree.

Kano turned to him and smiled. Old One did not smile back, but made a sign for Kano to follow.

Kano felt good inside. Today he had made it to the lake all by himself, and Old One had not turned him away. Now, for the first time, he felt the mosquitoes that had been around him all day. He was glad when Old One led him out from under the trees to a point of land where smoke from the fire and a light breeze kept them away.

Kano took off his packsack and sat down where Old One pointed. No word had passed between them since they met. Kano watched as Old One put fish on some sticks next to the fire. Old One's hair was long and gray and down over his shoulders; his body was short like a child's and his back was humped; his fingers were long and bony and bent with age; his face was almost black and covered with lines. He had no teeth. This man did not look like any of the old men who lived in the land of the Athabaskans; only his eyes told Kano he was not a Nakani. Old One's eyes were sad and told of loneliness.

As they began eating, Old One spoke his first words, "You wish to stay here by the lake?"

"Yes, how did you know this?" Kano asked.

Old One did not answer but went on, "You do not know what to do with the fear that comes inside you when you are in the forest alone?"

"That is true," Kano answered. "That is true, but how do you know this?"

"Long ago a boy like you lived in a village far from here in the land near the Eskimo. Like you, he did not know what to do with his fear. When he grew older he would not go out to hunt, and because he shamed his family and his village he was sent away and could never go back."

Old One sat looking into the fire and Kano asked, "And you were that boy?"

"Yes, I went to many other villages, but none would

let me stay." Old One stopped, then added, "It is the way of our people." Kano sat thinking and at last Old One went on, "Then I came here to this lake and learned to live with my fear."

"Old One, will you teach me what you have learned so I can go back to live with my people?"

"I will teach you all I know, but to know is not enough. Remember, your wish not to shame your family and your people must be strong. It must be stronger than your fear of the forest. Only then will you gladly go into the forest every day until your fear grows small. And then you will be a true Athabaskan Indian, a hunter who smiles when he talks of dying in the forest because the animals and birds who live there and who give life to his people make it a happy place."

The sun was now gone and the air had turned cold, but it was still light and Kano waited to learn more.

Old One reached over to put wood on the fire, and went on. "Your people do not like to talk of the Nakani because they are afraid this will make it angry. But you know the Nakani is called the 'Bad Indian' and is feared by all. You may know that even the great hunters among your people feel no shame in telling of their fear of the Nakani. And you may have been told that the Nakani can always be seen; that it takes the shape of a man or a woman. But I think you do not know that when the Nakani comes near you in the forest it does not always come to hurt you; that sometimes it comes near you because it is lonely."

Kano thought for a while, then answered, "I did not

know this. Always I was told to fear the Nakani because it helps the Giyeg—the father of devils."

"Yes, it sometimes does help the Giyeg, but it is not a devil. Now let me tell you of two other things that make your hunters fear the forest. And this fear they cannot show or tell about without bringing shame upon themselves."

The air was now still and many mosquitoes soon found the hands and faces of the two sitting and talking. Old One put rotten willow on the fire to make smoke that would help keep the mosquitoes away.

Kano asked, "What are these things that hunters fear most but cannot tell of? I have never been told of them."

"That is because even the great hunters do not wish to speak of them. But you must know them. And I will teach you ways that will make it easier for you to lose your fear of these things. Now it is already late."

"Please, Old One, tell me of these things," Kano begged.

Old One seemed glad to go on. "One of these things is the bear. It is the only animal in the forest that tries to kill men; even the greatest hunter's bow and knife cannot stop its teeth and claws. That is why the bear is called 'devil animal' and is hunted only in winter when it sleeps and by many men together. And that is why all hunters fear it even though they cannot say so."

When Kano heard Old One say this he knew why, on the caribou hunt last fall, his father had looked unhappy but had said nothing when Kano had told him that his fear of the bear had made him run away from where he had been told to wait. His father had felt great shame and could say nothing.

Kano sat and thought about this. At last he asked, "And what is this other thing that hunters fear?"

"It is the fear of getting lost. This is the greatest fear of all. Remember, the Nakani can be seen; it does not always wish to hurt, and stories are told of the Nakani being killed with arrows. The bear too can be seen. It too does not always wish to kill men, and hunters can always try to kill the bear. But when the hunter is lost he can do nothing; his brain goes empty and he becomes like a child again."

Kano thought about Old One's words. This had happened to him while he waited for the caribou, but he had not been lost.

Old One stood up slowly and threw more rotten willow on the fire. "That will keep the mosquitoes away until the wind comes toward morning and blows them away. In summer I live here; not under the trees. Here there is some wind. If you wish, you may live here with me. We can work together and you can use my canoe and gill nets. But for tonight, pull those spruce branches nearer the fire and sleep. Then tomorrow you must start trying to lose your fear of the Nakani. After that I will teach you how to lose the other two fears."

Kano was tired. As soon as he lay down he slept. The smoke from the fire and the mosquitoes did not bother him.

Kano did not wake up until the sun was high in the

sky. He sat up and remembered yesterday. He remembered Old One's words about the Nakani, about bears, and about getting lost.

Then he looked around for Old One; he was gone. The fire had burned low, but it was not out. He put fish left over from last night on a stick and warmed it. The fish tasted good. Now he was not afraid to be alone.

Time passed quickly as Kano sat thinking. After a long while two ravens flew low, landed in a tree nearby, and sat talking to each other. As he watched, he saw that the sun was already behind the trees. All day he had been alone, and not once had he been afraid. Maybe the Nakani had come while he sat thinking. Maybe his fear was getting smaller.

At last he thought of work. The gill net needed to be checked. But where was Old One? The canoe sat empty. Kano was alone. He thought once more of the work that must be done.

First he paddled the canoe over to the gill net, which was set in a stream where it flowed out of the lake. He took out four big whitefish. These he carefully put into the canoe and took back to camp. By the time the fish were cleaned and hung on the racks to dry, he was hungry. It was night again and the campfire needed more wood. Then Kano remembered the dried fish eggs Maya had packed, and he ate some of them mixed with oil.

Again he sat and thought, but now he thought about Old One. He remembered Maya's words about Old

One being a Nakani. Old One himself had said the Nakani can be seen, that they can be either men or women. Kano stood up and looked all around. He was alone, and now he saw that tonight it was darker than last night.

A few drops of rain touched his hands and face and he looked up to see that the sky was clouded over. Everything was still except for the buzzing mosquitoes. He put rotten willow on the fire and saw the smoke come up around him. The sharp smell filled his nose.

More rain fell. Now he felt it coming through his thick black hair. He picked up his pack, ran under a big spruce tree not far away, took his fishskin parka and pants out of the bag, and put them on.

Here he would be dry, but here the mosquitoes almost covered his face and hands. And here the trees and the cloudy skies made it seem almost dark. Kano looked behind him and saw, further back among the trees, Old One's winter house. Grass covered it except for the door. He ran to it, pushed back the skin over the door, and climbed carefully down into the hallway.

It was cold and damp and dark inside, but there were not so many mosquitoes. The Nakani did not like to come into houses. A fire would make it even better; the Nakani were afraid of fire.

Kano quickly climbed up and out the door. It did not take him long to find the smoke hole cover on top of the house and take it off. Next, he found dry sticks and threw them down the hole. Then he ran to the campfire, picked up burning sticks, and carried them into the house. Soon the fire burned brightly and lit up the small room.

Now he was safe. He would need more wood. For a while he sat very still, watching the fire and trying not to think about Maya, Old One, or the hunt he must make.

But at last he did think about these things. He thought about Napak and what would happen if Napak found out. He thought about the words of Old One: "Tomorrow you must start trying to lose your fear of the Nakani." Kano knew he was not trying to lose his fear of the Nakani. He was running away again.

Then more of Old One's words came back. "Your wish not to shame your family and your people must be strong; stronger than your fear." With these words in his mind Kano climbed back out of the doorway into the open air. And then he moved out from under the trees into the rain.

He pulled the hood of his fishskin parka over his head and sat down on the spruce branches. The fire was out, but he did not start a new one. His wish not to shame his family must be stronger than his fear.

The rain came down harder; everything was dark and wet. Kano's packsack was still under the tree; there it would stay dry. With his bow and arrows by his side and his knife in his hand, he sat, listened, and waited until sleep closed his eyes.

Something warm on Kano's face made him wake up. He sat up quickly, still holding his knife. His eyes were almost blinded. The rain and the clouds were gone. The bright sun had been shining down on him for many hours. Kano stood and slowly stretched himself. Last night he had made his fear smaller. He took off his fish-skin parka and pants and started the fire. He was hungry and there was much work to do.

Weeks passed and Old One did not come back. Kano wondered, but he was no longer afraid. Every day he worked hard. Every day whitefish filled the gill net and these he cleaned and put on the racks. He had to build more racks. He built a willow smokehouse and smoked some of the fish. He sewed fish skins together to hold the fish eggs and then he dug a hole and put them in it. And always he hoped, hoped Old One would come back and teach him more. He had lost his fear of the Nakani, and his fear of the bear was not so great, but he still was not sure about his fear of being lost.

Fewer mosquitoes and shorter days told Kano summer would soon end. More and more he thought of his family, but until he traveled alone in the forest away from any trail he would not be ready for the fall caribou hunt.

One morning Kano sat up with a start. It was still dark and something was wrong; something was close to him. As he slowly turned his head his hand picked up the knife he kept under his blanket. His heart pounded. Then his eyes saw the burning fire and close to it, smiling at Kano, sat Old One. Kano called out with happiness, "You came back!"

"Yes, you have lost your fear of the Nakani and now you are ready to learn more."

"But why did you stay away so long?" asked Kano.

"Fear of the Nakani is hard to lose. You needed much time," answered Old One.

"Now you are ready to think of your other fears. Today you must travel a long way and go where there are no trails to follow. But before you go, let me tell you two things."

Old One put more wood on the fire and then went on, "First, I will talk of the bears. Your father has told you that bears try to kill men only in the spring when they are very hungry and still cross from their long sleep. But you should know also that bears kill when you surprise them by coming close without their knowing it. Today, when you are walking in the forest, you should always be looking; and you should stop often to listen for sounds."

Kano moved closer so he could hear better. Old One warmed his hands by the fire as he said, "Now I will talk of getting lost. Athabaskan hunters do not get lost near their villages because they know all the little signs that tell them where they are—the trees, the trails, and all those things. But when they hunt far from home they watch too closely for the animals and they become lost. Today when you go you must always look around for the big signs—the mountains, the high hills, the valleys, and the lakes. Look to see how they stand in front of you, and then stop and look behind you to see how they stand when you have gone by them. Today there will be no small signs where you are going. There will be no trails, but you will not need them if you do as I have just told you."

Old One got up slowly. "Come, give me your pack, and while I put some food into it, you must think about what I have said."

When Old One had put the pack on Kano's back he said, "Remember, you will go to that far mountain and come back here. Do not walk in the dark. You must be back here tomorrow before night. But do not hurry; I will be waiting for you here."

Kano was glad as he started out. He had waited long for this day and now Old One had taught him all he needed to keep from being afraid.

But many things happened that day to test Kano. The first hours were hard. From the beginning there was no trail. Many willow bushes stood between Kano and the faraway mountain, and there were still many mosquitoes.

Kano stopped often: to rest, to listen for any sounds of the bear, and always to look up through the trees for the sun. The trees kept him from seeing the mountain, but if he kept the sun on his left side, Kano knew he would be going toward the mountain.

Time passed quickly and the sun was already moving down to meet the earth when Kano finally thought of food. He had come far and the sun had stayed with him all through the day. Now there were fewer trees and now he could see clearly the mountain that he must reach before turning back.

Kano kept going. The sun set and darkness began to fall over the land and still he had not come to the top of the mountain. But he had come far enough. And he had walked all day without getting lost. He was no longer afraid of the Nakani or of getting lost. Old One would want him to sleep here and start back down the mountain early in the morning.

Before opening his pack and getting settled for the night, Kano took one last look down the mountain. He could not see Old One's lake or the Anvik River. Then for the first time, he saw something that made his heart heavy. Far away, toward the Yukon River, clouds were starting to fill the night sky.

Kano had no need for a fire. He sat in the gathering darkness chewing on a smoked fish strip and thought about tomorrow. Tomorrow he would be going back down the mountain to the lake—back to Old One, and then back home. But tomorrow clouds might hide the sun. Kano fought the fear he felt growing inside of him. At last sleep came to his tired body.

The first light of day woke Kano and as his eyes opened he saw that clouds did cover the whole sky. He got up quickly and stuffed everything back into his packsack. His first thought was to start walking down the mountain before his fear could take over and make his brain go empty. The clouds were still high in the sky and he could still see the low hills and valleys that pointed the way to Old One's lake. Maybe by the time he got down into the trees, where he could no longer see the mountains, the sun would be back and show him the way once more.

Kano knew the sun would not come back to show

him the way. He stood there for a moment with his packsack on his back trying hard to think of something and trying hard not to let the fear in his heart get into his brain. Then Old One's words came back to him. "Do not hurry and always look for big signs."

Again he looked down the mountain toward Old One's lake. Again he saw the low hills falling off to where the Anvik River should be, and he saw the valleys between these hills.

Then he saw something else. In one of the valleys, a thin line of trees, taller than all the other trees around, ran along the floor of the valley and then seemed to curve around toward where Old One's lake should be. Kano knew this was the sign of a small stream. This stream was far to the right of the way Kano had come yesterday. It would be much longer if he went that way, but it would take him back to the lake. Now he would not need the sun. He had followed Old One's words and he had found a new sign that would keep him from getting lost.

Kano walked quickly down the mountain toward the small stream. All fear was now gone from his heart. He knew he would find his way back to Old One's lake.

It was already dark when Kano finally pushed through a clump of willow bushes along the stream he was following and found himself on the shore of a lake. A small fire not far away told him it was Old One's lake.

In a few moments Kano stood in front of that fire. He was tired and hungry, but he was also happy. He had won out over his fear.

Old One looked up at him and smiled, "I was worried for you today when I saw that clouds had hidden the sun from you. But I knew your wish not to shame your family would be greater than your fear."

The next morning, early, Kano stood again with his packsack on and his bow in his hands. Old One's eyes were sad as he said, "You will be a great hunter and your people will honor you."

Kano tried to keep the tears out of his eyes as he said, "And if I am so honored, I will tell my people who helped me when no one else could. I will always remember you. I will come here again some day and when I do it will be to repay you."

Kano turned quickly and as he walked away began thinking of those things he had learned from Old One.

That night he slept in his village and early the next morning, before the sun came up, he sat in his hunting canoe as the swift waters of the Yukon River carried him back to his summerhouse and to his family who were waiting there for him.

# 4

# The Caribou Hunt

The sun was not yet above the trees when Kano's canoe brushed against the gravel on the beach. In front of him, above the high bank, stood the summerhouse made of sprucewood planks. Next to it smoke curled and climbed toward the clear, blue sky. Kano stepped out and pulled his canoe after him. He heard only the swirl of the fast-moving water as he stretched and looked and listened.

The smell of fish mixed with the smell of ripe cranberries told him of the summer he had missed. He stood for a moment longer enjoying the thought of seeing once more the faces of his family. This was his home; his family had lived here as long as he could remember, and in the summers to come they would always live here.

The cold air pressed through his light caribou shirt, and far away he heard the wild cry of geese flying to warmer lands. Quickly he scrambled up the bank and looked around. Someone was in the smokehouse. He ran quickly toward it. As he did, Maya came out and started walking toward the trees in back of the summerhouse. Suddenly she stopped and turned around. Her hand went to her mouth as if to keep from crying out. Kano kept coming until he stood in front of her, staring. He had forgotten how beautiful she was. Her black hair fell back over her shoulders and her face and her dark eyes were shining with happiness.

Maya spoke first, "Kano, you are home, and you have grown taller."

Kano could not speak. His heart was too filled with happiness at seeing his sister whom he loved so much.

At last she took his hand and said, "Come, let us wake Father."

When they turned toward the house, their father was already standing, waiting, and watching. As they came near he said, "My son, your family thought of you often. Now you are home again." Then he spoke to Maya, "Now let us eat the special food you have been saving for this time!"

Before the day was over Kano found his place in the family work. All during the summer, fish had put themselves into the traps and nets of Kano's family. This winter there would be fish to give to the old people and to families without fathers. Everyone was happy and they sang as they worked. Grandmother sang as she filled baskets with ripe, red cranberries. Maya sang as she packed things and made ready to leave the summer home. Kano and his father sang "canoe songs" as they paddled their hunting canoes filled with fish upstream to the village and back again for another load until everything and everyone was back in the winter home.

Weeks passed and the time-of-the-falling-leaves was almost over on the morning Kano and his father stood by their hunting canoes ready to go up the Anvik River to hunt caribou. They would leave their canoes at the village called "Under-the-Rocks." From there they would take Kano's two dogs and go together to a camp high in the hills. There they would leave the dogs and each would go off alone to hunt. There Kano would be put to the test.

Each canoe carried only what was needed for the hunt; a dog, bow and arrows, and knife; a pack stick and pack line needed to carry out the caribou meat; and a little food that Maya had carefully fixed to eat on the way. Coming back from the hunt they hoped the canoes would be filled with caribou meat.

Kano sat in his canoe anxious to be off. He told Maya to hurry as she packed extra food next to him and away from the dogs. She smiled happily at him as she gave his canoe a push into the current. She was glad that he was no longer afraid to go on the hunt.

Although the canoes were lightly loaded, going against the current was hard work. Few people in the village used dogs. But Kano's father used them to carry meat during hunting and now, from time to time, they ran along the bank pulling at the end of a long line while

Kano and his father sat in the canoes and kept them away from the bank with their paddles. As he rested his tired arms, Kano was glad his father always found new ways to use the dogs.

Before night of the next day, they had reached their camp in the hills. This camp was only a willow hut near some running water. After carefully tying the dogs and giving them fish, Kano and his father went right to sleep.

The next morning, while it was still dark, they sat without a fire and ate the food Maya had sent. Then, standing outside the hut, Kano's father carefully checked Kano's bow and said to him, "Watch carefully where you go so you can find your way back, and stop often to look for animals. Here, where there are not so many trees, you can see better, but the animals can see better too." He stopped and then added, "And do not go so far that you cannot be back here at camp before dark."

Kano's father walked off to the north; Kano to the west. The sun's light now fell on the far mountains in front of him, but here in the lower hills he walked still in the shadows.

Kano remembered well Old One's words. He stopped at the top of a rise to look back and to the sides for large signs. Here, away from the thick forest, it was easier not to worry about the Nakani. Here, too, where there were fewer trees, it would be easier to see a bear. But it would still be hard to keep from getting lost. Hills were everywhere, and one looked much like the other. There were no lakes or rivers. The far mountains would help, but already clouds hung over the mountains in back of him. His father had said it might rain, and if it did, both the far mountains and the sun would be gone. Kano took one more look around and walked on.

All morning he hunted, watching for animals and always keeping in mind the way back to camp. The sky slowly filled with clouds, but Kano was not worried. He knew the hills better now, and they would show him the way back.

While Kano sat on a hillside eating smoked fish strips he saw his first caribou. The herd stood eating in a faraway valley next to some small trees. Quickly he put the fish strips away, picked up his bow, and hurried down the hill.

Kano was excited; he had a plan worked out. He would go around the next hill and come toward the caribou downwind so they could not smell him. The trees would let him get close enough for a good shot.

He walked quietly as he came close to where the caribou were eating. He reached the trees and his heart beat fast as he crawled and stopped and looked. Then, at last he saw them close by and still eating. One of them was very big; a bull, with antlers that seemed bigger than his whole body. This one lifted his head and looked around carefully. Kano froze. When the bull put his head down again, Kano fitted an arrow to his bow. He would try for the big bull; it would give much meat.

But before Kano could take careful aim, a squirrel

chattered in the tree right next to him, and with that sound the caribou started running. Kano took quick aim for the heart of the bull; he was close. But the aim was bad and Kano saw the arrow enter high on the caribou's right shoulder. He ran forward as he readied another arrow but now they were too far away.

The bull dropped behind the rest and Kano decided to give chase. He ran hard and seemed to be getting closer. The bull must be hurt or he would have left Kano far behind.

Kano was tired but so was the bull. Little by little the distance between them grew smaller. Kano saw nothing but the bull ahead of him. He must not lose it. Soon he would be close enough to try another shot.

But he did not get that second shot. He saw his first arrow fall away from the bull's shoulder and when this happened the animal picked up speed. Kano could not keep up. He fitted an arrow to his bow, dropped to one knee, and took aim. It was too late. The bull was far away and Kano's body was tired. The arrow missed its mark, flew far to one side, and dropped uselessly into the moss that covered the ground.

The chase was over; Kano had lost. At first he was too tired to care. He lay face down on the moss, breathing hard and resting.

Then slowly he felt anger. Why did this have to happen to him? He had done everything right. Something had kept the caribou from being his. Something had kept him from getting a caribou on this, his first hunt alone. He was angry.

Then something made him forget his anger. Suddenly he felt cold. He sat up and looked at the sky. It was not raining, but dreary, gray rain clouds hung low over the hills. Kano stood up quickly and looked around trying to find the way back to camp. As he stood there all alone, his hands began to shake and soon tears ran down his cheeks. Nothing showed him the way back to camp. He was lost.

In one short moment Kano forgot everything. He forgot what Old One had taught him. He forgot his family. And he forgot the one thing that might have helped him put down his fear: his wish not to shame his family and his people.

What happened next Kano could not afterward remember. When he finally did remember it was dark, it was raining, and he was lying on the grass underneath a tree. He was lost. His body was shaking but not from the cold. He knew he had been running a long time because his legs were tired, his hands were cut, his body was stiff and sore, and his pants and shirt were torn.

There were trees all around him; he must be in the forest. He thought of the Nakani and looked around for his bow and arrows. They were gone, he had lost them back there when his brain went empty.

Fear again filled his body, but he did nothing. He hurt, and he was too tired to move. He wished this were all a dream, that soon he might find himself awake in the willow hut with his father beside him and the dogs outside keeping watch. But it was not a dream and Kano knew it. Even the thought of Napak finding out and making fun of his fear did not matter. His body began to shake. He did not try to stop it. Tears ran down his cheeks; he did not try to stop them or wipe them away. He lay under the tree and heard the rain dripping from the leaves. At last he slept.

The hoot of an owl woke Kano with a start, or was it an owl? He sat listening; his body tense. It was very dark. Again came the *w-o-o-o* sound that he heard first as in a dream. It was long and low and full. It came from far away and he knew it was the sound his people used when looking for someone who is lost. This sound was used because it could be heard far away.

Kano stood up and gave the call back. He listened, and after a while he heard it again. It seemed closer. It must be his father.

The call was given many more times. Each time Kano called back. It was a long wait but he was no longer afraid. He tried not to think about all that had happened. But he did, and now his body filled with shame.

When the sound was very close Kano called, "Father," and when his father called back, "Yes," he ran that way. At last they stood facing each other. Kano said nothing and even in the dark he could not look at his father. He put his head down and waited.

After what seemed like forever to Kano, his father spoke, "It will soon be light. Let us wait here until then; I will listen to you."

At first, Kano would say nothing. He could not say the words that needed to be said. His father waited. At last, little by little, Kano told everything and he did it without crying, which would have shamed his father even more.

Again there was no talk. And again, to Kano, it seemed forever before his father said, "You have brought shame on yourself and on our family, but you did try. You did go on this caribou hunt as you were told to do. You will not be sent away in shame from your family and your village."

Kano wished to thank his father for understanding him, but his shame was too great.

The morning light came through the trees before Kano's father spoke again. "The white men in the place by the big water where I go to trade have asked me many times to send a boy from my village to live with them. They say this boy could then go back and forth between the villages of his people and the white man's place to help trade furs for the things of the white man."

When he stopped, Kano asked quietly, "And you wish me to be that boy?"

His father answered, "You must choose. You will not be sent to the white man's village unless you wish to go."

Kano did not know for sure why his father would let him go to the white man's village to learn their ways. He did not know for sure why he wished to go, but he did. Without waiting, he answered, "Yes, Father, I wish to go." He did know this would bring less shame on his family.

There was sadness in his father's voice as he said, "When the snows come I will go to the white man's village called 'St. Michael.' While I am there I will talk to the white men about this. Then, when it is time for spring camp, I will go to trade again. This time I will take you with me and you will live with the white men."

It was now light and they started back to camp. Kano's father had killed a caribou the day before and had the meat already at camp. With the help of the dogs they were able to carry all the meat down to the village called "Under-the-Rocks" without going back a second time.

That same day the waters of the Anvik River carried their canoes swiftly toward home. There was caribou meat for the winter in both canoes. The day was warm and filled with sunlight that splashed on the waters as they moved along; but in Kano's heart there was shame and sadness. And in the canoe ahead Kano did not hear his father singing the "canoe song."

# 5

# The Stranger

Winter came to Anvik soon after the caribou hunt. The days grew shorter, the nights turned bitter cold, and then one morning the village awoke and found the ground covered with snow. Winter came so quickly that the river did not have time to freeze over, but floating ice could be seen everywhere.

Some of the old people of the village said it was too early for the snow to stay; the sun would come out and soon the snow would be gone.

But this did not happen. Instead the sky stayed cloudy, and an icy north wind could be heard roaring down the Yukon River on the other side of the hill. Three days it roared, and when it stopped the sun came out again. The air stayed cold and the rivers were frozen over. Winter had come to Anvik.

During those days, Kano noticed that his father

spent little time in the Kashim. He seemed to be always busy getting things ready for his trading trip to St. Michael. And Kano could not help noticing that his father did not smile the way he used to, before the caribou hunt.

Then, on the evening before the trip to St. Michael, Kano was helping cover the loved-fire in the Kashim when he heard one of the old men say to his father, "Some day soon your son will be one of our best hunters."

His father did not answer, but soon after that he quietly picked up his parka and slipped outside. Now Kano knew why his father kept away from the other men in the Kashim.

Kano put on his parka and left too. As he stepped out into the cold night air, he could see his father walking slowly away from him toward their house.

Kano followed him into the house and when he came inside, his father had already taken off his parka and stood watching Maya as she sat sewing. Without first taking off his parka, Kano sat down and watched Maya too.

Maya put down her sewing. She looked at her father and then at Kano. She asked, "Do you two not wish to sleep in the Kashim tonight?"

Her father answered, "I must leave early tomorrow morning. It is best I sleep here so I do not wake the men in the Kashim."

He started to move away, but Kano stopped him by saying, "Please, Father, let me say this before you go."

His father sat down and waited. Everything was quiet except for Grandmother's gentle snoring. Kano struggled for words that would lessen the hurt in his father's heart. "Father, the shame I have brought to you and to this family is great. It is hard for you when the old men in the Kashim tell you what a great hunter your son will be."

No one spoke as Kano stopped for a moment, and then went on, "Tell them now, Father, that I am going to live in the place of the white man, and take me with you now. Then, when you come back here, no one will talk to you about me, and this will make your hurt less."

When Kano finished, Maya did not give her father a chance to answer. "Father, he cannot go now. Grandmother and I need him here while you are gone."

"Yes, Maya, you are right, Kano is needed here."

Then he looked at Kano and said, "But, Kano, there is another, more important, reason why you must not go with me now. The hurt that you speak of is also in your heart. You feel it now more than you will when the time-of-melting-snow comes and you go with me to the white man's place."

He stopped, but Kano and Maya saw that he had more to say, so they waited. At last he said, "Now, at the time that you feel the hurt most, you should be here with your family, not far away in the place of the white man."

Maya wiped the tears from her eyes as she heard these words. Kano sat and said nothing. He was glad his father knew there was hurt in Kano's heart too.

No more words needed to be said, and the next morning, as the dogs and sled stood ready, Kano and Maya saw their father turn and smile at them. Then he called to the dogs and they strained to start the heavy load on its way.

Kano and Maya stood side by side in the clear, cold morning air. They watched until the sled and driver moved out of sight around the first bend in the river.

After his father left, Kano kept himself busy and stayed away from the Kashim. He went there only to sleep. He did not want to see the old men smiling at him and to hear them say to each other, "That boy will soon be our best hunter."

One day, before the time-of-the-long-nights, Maya asked Kano to take food to the sister of their grand-mother, the one they called "Auntie." This Auntie was very old, but she wished to live alone. Her house was to the north on the Yukon River, but not far from Anvik. Many people stopped in on their way by her place: some to see if she needed anything, others just to visit in her warm, friendly home.

Kano was off early. His two dogs hurried along the river trail while he stood with one foot on each sled runner and held on with both hands. The sun was just moving up over the trees across the wide river. It would not go much higher that day and the air would stay cold. But Kano did not mind. He was warm in his long parka and mittens and in his caribou pants with the hair turned inside up against his skin.

Kano liked going along the Yukon in winter. Here

the whole world seemed asleep under a thick blanket of snow. Nothing but Kano and his dogs moved on the wide, frozen river, or among the tall spruce trees that lined its banks. All was quiet except for the creaking of the sled as it moved over the rough ice, and the panting of the dogs as they ran. Here there was no chance of getting lost. And here, in winter, there was no Nakani, because the Nakani feared leaving its tracks in the snow.

Kano was thinking of these things when the sled and dogs rounded a bend, and there, sitting under three tall spruce trees, he saw Auntie's house. Smoke coming out of the smoke hole told Kano she had slept late and was still making breakfast.

As he came closer he saw a team of dogs, still hitched to the sled, standing in front of the house. This meant Auntie had visitors. Kano did not want to go in. He would have turned back, but then he thought of Maya. She had told him to bring this food to Auntie and she would send him right back if he had not done it. Sometimes Kano did not like having a sister who acted like a mother.

He stopped his dogs far enough away from the other team so they wouldn't fight, and then tied his sled to a tree. As he walked toward the house, Kano looked at the other sled and dogs. He had not seen them before.

Then, as he climbed down into the hallway, he bumped into things to tell the people inside a visitor wished to come in. As soon as he did this, he heard Auntie ask, "Are you coming in?"

Kano answered, "Yes."

Coming from outside, Kano's eyes were not used to the dim light. As he stepped through the inside doorway he could see Auntie sitting by the fire.

Her eyes could not make out who he was, but when he said, "Auntie, Maya sends you some of her special food," she smiled and answered, "Yes, Kano, please sit down here by the fire."

As Kano moved to sit down he had time to look at the visitor. But he was not quite ready for what he saw. Sitting across the fire from Auntie was the biggest man Kano had ever seen. And this man's skin was almost white—the color of salmon bellies. His clothes, except for his parka, which he still had on, were different too. They were not made by Athabaskans, or even by the Eskimo.

Kano had never seen a white man before and he could not help staring. He especially could not help staring at the man's face. It was covered with red hair from his neck all the way around his mouth and up to his nose.

Kano remembered what his grandmother had told him. She said these men have white skins because they come from under the ground, from the land of the dead. Kano wondered.

Then Kano thought about the place of the white man called "St. Michael" where his father had gone to trade. He thought of having to live with these white men, and of having to learn their ways. "What would it be like?" he wondered.

At last the man spoke in the words of Kano's people, "My name is Ivan. I am Russian."

Kano was not able to answer until he looked into the man's eyes. Then he forgot all the things that made this stranger so different. Those eyes spoke of friendship and Kano understood. He said, "I am Kano."

Auntie had already filled a bowl with soup and handed it to Kano as she said, "Here, you are cold. You must have some warm soup."

As Kano took the bowl, she went on, "This Russian comes to tell us of the great sickness they call smallpox. We know it has already visited the Eskimo who live on the Yukon down from us. He thinks it will soon be here, and he comes to give us medicine that he says will keep the sickness away."

Auntie stopped and waited for Kano to speak. When he didn't, the white man called Ivan looked at Kano as he said, "But the one you call 'Auntie' will not take this medicine."

Before Kano could say anything, Auntie spoke again, "Yes, because the Eskimo say the white men gave their medicine to people, but still they died."

Ivan turned back to Auntie and said, "That is why the medicine must be given before the sickness comes. If it is given after the sickness has already come to a village, it will keep some of the people from dying, but not all."

Auntie was still not satisfied. She said, "Our own medicine man is called to make medicine when one of our people is sick."

"But this sickness comes from the white man, and the white man's medicine must be used to keep it away."

Auntie's answer showed she still did not trust the Russian. "I have lived all this time following the ways of my people. I will not change now."

Kano sat listening to all this and wondered. He wanted to believe the Russian. Kano's father traded with the white men and brought sharp knives and other things which helped his people. Then why couldn't his people take this medicine from the white men too?

Kano knew this was different. The things his father brought that changed the ways of his people, like the sharp knives, could be seen and used. But this medicine, no one knew how it worked. People feared that which they did not understand.

Kano's thoughts were ended when he heard Ivan ask him, "And you, Kano, you are young. Will you trust the white man's medicine?"

Kano feared the white man's medicine just as he still feared getting lost in the forest. To his own surprise, he found himself saying to this stranger, "I fear this new medicine."

Ivan shook his head with understanding as he answered, "Your people and mine all fear things. Not always the same things, but fear is always there. Fear does not bring shame, unless it keeps us from doing the things we should do."

Kano looked away as he heard Ivan's last words. He knew his old fear was keeping him from becoming a great hunter for his people.

Then he heard Ivan say, "Maybe you should take the medicine in order to help your people. If you take it, and do not get the sickness, then your people will take it too, and they will not die if someone brings the sickness to your village."

Kano heard these words and then looked into Ivan's eyes and knew what he would do. He said, "I fear the medicine, but I do not believe you would give it to me if it would give me this sickness called smallpox. I will take the medicine."

Ivan nodded his head and said nothing, but again his eyes spoke and Kano understood.

Ivan went outside to get his medicine box. While he was gone, Auntie said, "Kano, you should not do this until you speak to your father."

"My father has gone to the white man's place to trade."

"Then you should wait until you speak to the old men in the Kashim."

"Auntie, if I wait, my fear may grow too strong again. Then I will not take this medicine. I know I should take it because it will help our people. If I take it, they will soon find out if it is good or bad medicine."

Ivan came back in and Auntie said nothing more.

As Ivan took off his parka and started unwrapping the fur from around his medicine box he said, "Kano, you must take off your parka and pull up one of your sleeves. I will put a drop of the medicine on your arm and then scratch it into your skin with a special needle."

Ivan saw Kano's face when he heard the word "needle" and smiled as he said, "Do not worry, I will not stick the needle into your arm. I will only scratch lightly. It will feel like someone tickling you."

Kano felt better. He still remembered how much it had hurt when holes were made at each corner of his mouth so he could wear bone plugs. He himself had asked to have it done so he could show off to the other boys. Then, when they started making the holes and it hurt so much, he wanted to change his mind, but the men in the Kashim would not let him. Ever since that time he did not wish to come close to any kind of needle.

Ivan went on getting the medicine ready as he said, "It is easy to put this medicine into your arm. I want you to watch everything carefully so you can help me if the people in your village take the medicine. Also, they might fear it less if you are the one putting it into their arms."

Kano did watch everything carefully. As Ivan promised, it did not hurt. When it was all over, he knew he could give the medicine to someone else.

Kano got the food for Auntie from the sled while Ivan put the medicine box back into its warm fur cover. But Ivan did not put it away before asking Auntie once more if she would take the medicine.

She still shook her head and said, "No."

Then both said good-bye to Auntie and set off for Anvik.

It was still early afternoon when they arrived in front of the Kashim, but it was already dark. Kano suggested they go right in so that Ivan could talk to the men before the fire for the sweat bath was started. Kano and some of the other older boys could unhitch the dogs and feed them later.

Ivan was happy to do this since he hoped to give the medicine to the people of Anvik that very night and then move on down river to the next village in the early morning.

When they stepped through the inner doorway of the Kashim they found most of the men still working on different things they were making. The smell of cut willow and other wood was strong in the air.

When a few of the men looked up and saw who was with Kano, a murmur spread through the big room. Soon everyone was looking at the stranger. Only twice before had a white man been in this Kashim.

Kano spoke first. He told how he had met the stranger who wanted now to speak to the men in the Kashim.

Ivan began to speak in the words of the people and Kano heard him tell about the sickness called smallpox: how last year it had come to the Eskimo who lived to the south, and about the medicine he brought that would keep the people of Anvik from dying if someone should bring the smallpox here.

When Ivan finished, an old man at the front of the Kashim stood up and asked, "We know that many people are dying among the Eskimo. But why do you tell us the sickness will come here?"

Ivan answered, "This smallpox moves quickly. It is carried in the clothes and even in the cough of one who is himself not sick, but who has touched one who has the sickness."

No sooner had Ivan finished saying this than a young man stood up and shouted at him, "We have been told the white men carry this sickness with them in the medicine they bring. Is it not true that people who have taken your medicine have died?"

Other young men stood up and shouted, "Yes, it is true!"

Ivan waited until the shouting had died down and then Kano heard him trying to explain how the medicine worked, and why the medicine must be taken early.

When he finished explaining, many shook their heads showing that they did not believe. No one spoke for a while, then another of the old men stood up and said, "The medicine man of our people lives nearby on the Anvik River. If the sickness comes he will know what to do."

Ivan answered him, "But this is a sickness that is new to your people. Your medicine man will need the help of the white man's medicine."

Again one of the younger men stood and shouted, "Yes, you speak the truth. The sickness is new to our people. It is new because the white man brings it to us. The white man wants our people to die so he can live on our lands and fish in our rivers and hunt in our forest. We want the white man to go. We do not want his medicine."

Now many of the men were standing and shouting, "Yes, go! And take your medicine."

Kano looked at Ivan and saw that he did not know what else to do. Then he saw one of the old men walk slowly to where he and Ivan stood. It was the one called "Killer-of-bears," the one who had given his lucky animal song to Kano and who had been honored at Kano's Feast of the First Hunt. As he walked, the shouting stopped and the Kashim grew quiet again.

Before Killer-of-bears was able to get to where they stood, Kano slipped off his parka and said, "This stranger has come from far away and has spent many days on the trail. I believe he wishes to help our people."

Then he pulled up his sleeve to show the mark on his arm and said, "This mark shows that I have taken the medicine. I took it to show my people it is good medicine."

Killer-of-bears now stood next to Kano and Ivan, but before he could speak, Kano saw Napak coming toward them. He was looking straight at Kano as he shouted, "You! It is you who brought this white man into our Kashim and it is you who have taken the white man's medicine without first asking the old men. Now you tell us what we should do. You forget, it is your work to become a good hunter, not to tell the old men what is best for our people."

Again there was shouting and now almost everyone was standing. But when Killer-of-bears raised both his hands, everyone sat down and waited.

When all was quiet he spoke. "Enough! The old men will now meet. No more talk of the medicine until we finish."

He walked back to where the other old men waited and Kano and Ivan sat down on one of the benches.

Kano was angry because the men had listened to Napak, because they did not understand why he had taken the medicine.

The men in the Kashim did not have to wait long. Killer-of-bears came up again and spoke. "Our people will not take the white man's medicine. Our people have their own medicine man."

He stopped to look at Kano, then said, "Kano must be punished for taking the medicine without asking first. He will not again come into the Kashim until the old men have met with his father."

Then he turned to Ivan and said, "Our Kashim is always open to strangers. But because you have given the medicine to this young boy without coming to the Kashim first, you cannot stay."

No more was said. Ivan left the Kashim and Kano followed him.

Outside, the air seemed colder than before. A full moon spread its white light over everything.

Kano spoke first, "You may stay at our house, and start out in the morning."

Ivan answered, "No, Kano, I have brought you enough trouble. It will only make the young men more angry if I stay. It is still early, the moon is out, and the trail is clear."

Kano helped him bring the sled and dogs around onto the trail.

When Ivan stood on the sled runners, ready to go, he

said, "Your people have reason to be angry. The white men brought this sickness that kills so many. And they do not understand that the medicine should be taken before the sickness comes."

Kano asked, "Do all the villages turn away your medicine?"

"No, some do not. I will go down the river now to where the Innoko flows into the Yukon. Then I will come up the Innoko visiting villages there too. Remember, the river lies only a half-day's travel to the east. If you need me, come across to the Innoko. You will find me there in one of the villages."

Kano wanted to say so many things but he could not find the words.

At last Ivan said, "Do not be sad, Kano. You did right. Maybe the old men will change their minds as the days pass and they see my medicine did not make you sick."

With this said, he called to the dogs and was gone.

Kano walked slowly to his own two dogs. They must be unhitched and fed.

Then he would have to go in and tell Maya.

# 6

## The White Man's Sickness

The news of the Russian coming to the Kashim, and why he came, traveled quickly to every house in the village. But all that was said was not true. Some said that the Russian was sent away because he did not bring gifts. Others said that the great sickness was already in the village.

And so it was with the news about Kano. It too traveled quickly, and some of the things told were not true.

Kano told Maya and Grandmother all that had happened, both at Auntie's and in the Kashim. Both the women felt that taking the medicine was a brave thing to do, and that it was right because Kano did it to help his people. This made him feel better, but he knew there were others who thought he did wrong.

Both Maya and Grandmother also felt that the people should use the new medicine, especially if days passed and Kano did not get sick. Both of them said they would talk about this with the other women in the village.

In the days that followed, Kano did not get sick, but they were unhappy days for him. The new sled he was building was in the Kashim. He could not go there to work on it, even at night. The house, during the day, was a place where the women come to visit, and he did not want to be there when they came. But worst of all he worried. He worried about the sickness coming to his village and what would happen to Maya and to Grandmother.

Every day he would hitch up his two dogs as soon as it was light and then he would stay out until the sun set. Sometimes it was already dark when he came back to the house and then Maya would scold him.

As the days passed, the people of Anvik forgot about the sickness and about the white man's medicine. Many of the women agreed with Maya and Grandmother that the medicine should be used. But they did not talk to their men about it.

With Kano it was different. Every day that went by made him believe even more that sickness would come to his village before the winter passed. And every day he tried to think of something he could do to get the people of his village to take the new medicine.

He remembered what Ivan had said about finding him in one of the villages on the Innoko River. The trail across to the Innoko was not used often. Maybe once or twice, toward the time-of-melting-snow, the people from there would come across to Anvik to trade furs for meat and fish.

Kano decided to spend his time breaking the trail so it would be ready if his people ever wanted to get the medicine. One day he went over halfway across to the Innoko. It made him feel good to know that he could go out and make his own trail without being always afraid of getting lost. But still, this was not the same as going out by himself in the summer. In the summer it was much easier to get lost because there were no tracks in the snow to follow back to where he started. And in the summer there was always the Nakani.

That night, Kano told Maya what he had been doing. He said that now he would like to go all the way across to the Innoko. He would stay overnight in the Kashim at Shageluk, which was the first village on the other side. Then he would come back the next day.

Grandmother had been sitting by the fire listening as Kano talked to Maya, and she said, "The people of the Innoko are a tribe of our people, but we do not visit each other unless there is a need to. Long ago some of their men took meat from our caches while our men were out hunting. That is not the way of our people."

Kano answered, "But, Grandmother, that was long ago. Do you think the people of Shageluk will not invite me to stay in their Kashim for just one night?"

Now Maya spoke, "Kano, why do you wish to go there? The days are so short now."

Kano answered, "It will be a good test for me. I wish to show Father that I can go out by myself without being afraid."

Maya smiled at him, "That is good. Father will be

glad. But is that the only reason?"

Kano did not answer and Maya then asked, "What is the other reason?"

"The Russian, Ivan, told me he would come up the Innoko from the Yukon and stop at each village as he came. I hope to find him and to bring him back with me."

Then Grandmother asked, "And what good would that do?"

"This time I would not take him to the Kashim. I would bring him here and ask you both to take the medicine. Remember, I have had the medicine in me for many days now and it has not hurt me."

Neither Maya nor Grandmother spoke, so Kano added, "And both of you have said you believe the medicine should be used."

Maya said, "Yes, but the old men in the Kashim have said the medicine is not to be used."

Kano looked at Grandmother as he answered, "Perhaps if the old men of the Kashim are told how the women feel then perhaps they will let the medicine be used."

Grandmother said nothing, but Maya did. "We will think about it for a day. Feed your dogs well and let them rest. Tomorrow you must take food to Auntie and then, when you come back, we will talk more of this."

The next morning Kano was out of the house and well down the trail almost before it was light. The wind was blowing down the river and he felt the cold on his face even with his parka hood up. He was glad he was not going across to the Innoko today.

Still he felt good. He was sure Maya would let him go to the Innoko, and if she did, he would not come back until he brought Ivan with him.

This time as he came near Auntie's house he saw that the smoke hole cover was still in place. She must still be sleeping, he thought.

He quickly tied the sled in a place where the dogs would be out of the wind. Then he climbed down into the hallway. As he did this, the sound of a drum reached his ears and then he heard singing.

Kano's heart began to pound. It was the drum of the medicine man. Auntie was sick. Kano moved through the hallway into the house without waiting for anyone to call out to him first.

Auntie was lying on the bench bed near the fireplace and the medicine man was sitting next to her with his back to Kano.

From where he stood Kano could see only Auntie's face. And for the first time he saw this sickness Ivan called smallpox. He could hardly believe his eyes.

Auntie's face was puffed up and covered with big yellow boils. Some of these boils had broken and the smell from them filled the room. Kano felt sick but he could not turn away.

As he stood looking, a hand touched his arm and he turned quickly to see who it was.

A woman stood next to him. He did not know her. She whispered, "You must go. The medicine man says this woman has the great sickness. He has brought me to care for her. He wants no one else to come into this house."

As she finished saying this, she pushed Kano gently back through the doorway. He stepped through it without looking back. Once outside he ran to untie the sled and then hurried the team toward home.

As he stopped in front of the house and began to tie the sled, Maya heard the dogs and stuck her head out of the doorway to see why Kano was back so soon.

Kano brushed past her and climbed quickly down into the house. Maya followed close behind, and asked "What happened?"

"Auntie has the great sickness!"

"How do you know this?"

"The medicine man says so. He was there and he brought with him a woman to help care for her."

"But, Kano, she is our Auntie. If she is sick, I must go to care for her."

"No, the medicine man will let no one else in the house."

Maya then asked, "Does the village know of this?"

"I do not know, but someone must have sent for the medicine man."

Then Kano turned to the thing that he had been thinking about all the way back from Auntie's. "Maya, I must leave now to find Ivan. You and Grandmother must talk to the women so they will be ready to take the medicine when he and I return."

"But, Kano, you cannot go today. You saw how the wind was blowing down the Yukon. On the other side it will be just as bad. You know there are no trees to break the wind and the blowing snow will not let you see the trail."

"Maya, I must go. There is no time to wait."

Maya thought for a moment, then said, "Father would be pleased to hear you say that, but he would not want you to go on a day such as this. Let us ask one of the men to go."

"No, do not tell the men. They might not let anyone go."

"But Kano, how will you keep to the trail when the blowing snow will not let you see it?"

"Father has told me that when the wind hides the trail, keep the wind always in the same place as you go. The trail across to the Innoko is straight. I shall keep the wind always on my left side."

"And if this does not work? The wind will cover up your tracks and you will not be able to follow them back here."

"I have thought of that too. I can always let the dogs have their way. They will come straight home."

Maya was still worried, but she said, "Go then. Father has taught you well. But first you must eat. Warm soup is waiting. And I will give you the fish eggs I keep hidden away so you cannot find them. While you eat, I shall give your dogs the best food I can find."

Kano ate quickly. He was not hungry, but it would be many hours before he and the dogs would eat again. Before he could leave, Maya made him put on a heavier parka and heavier boots and mittens. At last he was off.

As Maya stood watching him go, she wiped tears from her eyes. She was sorry Grandmother had slept through all this and could not see him standing tall on the sled as it dropped down the bank toward the Yukon River.

The first hours passed by quickly for Kano. The dogs ran well and kept to the trail even when Kano himself could not see it. He knew they were going straight because the wind stayed always on his left side.

There were no trees along the trail, only a few low bushes. The wind would be strong all the way across until they came to the trees that grew along the Innoko which was named "In-the-woods-river." But Kano and the dogs did not mind the wind as long as they did not have to face into it.

Now and then Kano saw a bush he had marked on one of his earlier trips. These signs told him everything was going well. He was still on the trail.

It was not until he came to the spot where he had turned back the day before that something happened.

The dogs slowed down and then stopped. Kano called out to them and at the same time pushed the sled ahead. The lead dog moved around until his back was to the wind. Kano then walked to the front and pulled the dogs around until the wind was again blowing from the left.

Again he called out, but now the they would not move at all. The leader just kept looking back.

Kano didn't know what to do next, but he did not feel fear. There was no trail ahead; still he was not lost.

The dogs would always take him back home.

At last he decided to lead them for a while until they got used to walking without a trail. It was hard work. They held back and Kano had to keep pulling at the lead dog's collar to keep them moving at all.

After struggling along for a time, Kano again moved to the back of the sled and tried to get the dogs to go out on their own. They still would not do it.

Then as Kano stood there thinking of what to try next, a strange thing happened. The wind began to die down and then stopped, except for short gusts that seemed to blow from one side then another.

Now Kano had lost the one marker that had kept him going toward the Innoko. He looked around. The snow had stopped blowing and he could see, but not very far. Low clouds covered the mountains that he used when he broke trail the day before. Everywhere he turned everything looked the same—flat land covered with drifted snow with a few willow bushes sticking up here and there.

He could see no sign of a trail. With no wind or mountains to use as markers, there seemed no way of keeping on a straight line and of reaching the Innoko.

More and more Kano thought of turning back. And as he did, he thought of reasons why he should. It was true, he would not get lost if he kept going. Because now, without the wind, he could follow his tracks back to this spot. But he would be wasting time. Instead, if he let the dogs take him home now, some man from the village who knew the way better could go to the Innoko and find Ivan.

Then he thought of another reason for going back. What would happen if he went on looking for the trail and then the wind started to blow again? It might not blow from the north this time, but it would wipe out his tracks. Then what if the dogs were no longer able to find their way home?

This last thought brought back Kano's old fear of getting lost. But this time his brain did not go empty. Instead there came into his mind a picture of Maya lying on her bed, under a caribou blanket, with her face all puffed up and covered with yellow boils. Some of these boils she had scratched open and the smell was bad.

With this picture in his mind, Kano walked quickly around to the front and started leading the dogs again. He was not sure he could keep going straight toward the river, but he would not stop trying.

Then, as he walked and looked for some sign of the trail, something wonderful happened. Kano saw something that would be a marker for him instead of the wind. It was something his father had not taught him. The north wind had blown the snow into long, narrow drifts that made lines across the path Kano had to follow to get to the Innoko. If he cut right through these lines with his sled he would be going straight to the river.

Kano started out again and found his new idea worked. He also noticed that the dogs were moving along behind him without being pulled, as if they trusted him.

Now Kano had time to look around, and as he did he saw that it would soon be dark. If he did not reach the river before dark, he would have to dig into the snow and roll up in the caribou blankets Maya had sent along and then wait for morning.

He tried again to get the dogs to move out on their own, and this time they did. Kano stood on the back of the sled and helped them by keeping one foot on the sled runner and pushing with the other. Soon the dogs were running fast over the hard, drifted snow.

Because the sky was clouded over, Kano knew it would be getting dark sooner than the day before. He kept looking ahead, looking for tall spruce trees that would tell him he had reached the Innoko. But all he saw was more snow.

Then, all at once, the dogs started running even faster. At first Kano thought they were chasing a rabbit and he quickly made sure the sled was still cutting through the snow drifts. It was. There could be only one other reason why the tired dogs would start running faster. They knew a village was near. A few minutes later he saw spruce trees ahead. Not long after that he pulled up in front of the Kashim at Shageluk. Kano had made it across. Now he must find Ivan.

In the Kashim they told him the Russian had not yet come to their village. They had heard he was giving medicine to the people in the next village down called "The-river-goes-around-it." They invited him to sleep overnight in the Kashim, but he would not stay.

It was dark as he left Shageluk but the trail was well

used and the dogs had rested at the Kashim. Kano was tired now, and hungry, and he did not help by pushing, but the dogs did not seem to mind.

Kano did not know how late it was when he finally reached the village called "The-river-goes-around-it." When he came to the Kashim in that village, he knew he did not have to go any farther. There, next to the door, he saw Ivan's sled.

Kano tied his own sled and went inside. The Kashim was quiet and some of the men were already lying down. He had no trouble picking out Ivan with red hair covering almost all of his face.

When Ivan saw Kano, a smile came to his face and he hugged him. Kano felt strange. He did not know what to do, but he knew that the Russian was glad to see him.

Kano told all that had happened. Then, when he asked Ivan to go back with him, the older man shook his head sadly, "I cannot go with you now. I must give the medicine to the people here and then go on to the other villages."

He saw Kano's face and went on, "But, Kano, you do not need me. I have shown you how to give the medicine. You can take some of it back with you and give it to your people."

Kano was afraid, and as he looked at Ivan his eyes begged him to change his mind.

Ivan only looked at Kano and said, "That which I ask you to do is not easy. But I know you can do it, and I know you will."

Kano said nothing. He knew Ivan was right.

Then, when Kano suggested starting back that same night, Ivan would not hear of it. He said Kano must be fed and put to bed. He, Ivan, would unhitch and feed Kano's dogs and get the medicine ready. In the morning he would wake Kano early, feed him again, and have him on his way home before daylight.

Then Ivan's whole face smiled as he said, "This I must do because you are my friend."

Kano smiled back. He was glad his friend was making him eat and rest before starting back.

After Kano had eaten, he lay down. The sounds around him made him think of his own Kashim, and sleep came quickly. And as he slept, thoughts about the wind and the trip and the trail danced in his head.

# 7

## Bringing Help

**K**ano woke when he felt a hand touch his shoulder. Then he heard Ivan whisper, "Time to go."

The Kashim was still dark except for the small lamp Ivan had lit. Kano dressed quickly. And while he ate the food Maya had sent with him, he watched Ivan show him once more how the medicine was to be given.

"The needle must stay in this box until you are ready to use it. And the medicine: keep it wrapped in the furs when you travel. It must not freeze."

Then Ivan went on to explain what should be done to keep the sickness from being given to others. "The clothes of the sick person must be burned."

As Kano heard these last words he remembered again why he must hurry back to his village. Perhaps the sickness had already come to others, besides Auntie. He tried hard not to think of Maya.

When Ivan was done explaining they left the Kashim. As they came outside, Kano saw that his dogs were already hitched to the sled. Ivan helped him put the medicine into the sled so it would keep warm and not fall out.

Then it was time to go. Ivan put his hands on Kano's shoulders and looked down at him. He smiled and said, "Some day soon I will come to visit your village again."

Kano smiled back and turned to go. As the sled moved out, he heard Ivan say, "May the Great Spirit of your people and mine go with you this day."

The trip home was easy. The clouds were gone and the sun came up as Kano passed through Shageluk. As the dogs left the river and started across the flats, they seemed to know they were going home, and their feet moved even faster along the trail.

The tracks from the day before were still there so Kano had little to do but worry about Maya and Grandmother and the rest of his people.

By the time Kano came close to home, the sun had dropped behind the mountains on the other side of the Yukon River, but he could still see Anvik Hill with the tall spruce trees standing on top of it. The dogs, too, knew they were almost home and started running faster again.

When the dogs finally stopped in front of Kano's house he did not take time to unhitch them or even tie the sled. Picking up the medicine box, he quickly climbed down into the hallway and stepped into the house.

Maya and Grandmother were both there, sitting by the fire. Maya gave a cry of surprise and then, when she saw he was alone, she asked, "But, Kano, where is the Russian?"

"He could not come," Kano answered, "but he has given me the medicine and has shown me how to give it." Then he asked, "Are you and Grandmother well? How is Auntie? Has the sickness come to anyone else?"

"As you see, Grandmother and I are well. Auntie still lives, but the medicine man will let no one see her."

Grandmother went over to Kano while Maya was talking, and she asked,"And you will give us the white man's medicine?"

"Yes, Grandmother. But Maya has not told me, do others have the sickness?"

Grandmother answered him, "Yes, but only one. To keep the sickness from going to others, the medicine man has told the women to stay in their houses, and the men to stay in the Kashim. The women fear for their children and will come here to take the medicine as soon as you can give it."

"Then let us start now," said Kano. "Maya, make a place on the bench bed for the medicine box. Then let me give you the medicine first so you can go out and bring in the women and children."

Maya helped find a place for the box where Kano would reach it easily. Then, as she stood holding out her arm, she saw Kano pick up the needle. She looked away.

Kano saw this but said nothing. He quickly put a drop of the medicine on her arm and scratched it in gently.

When it was done, he asked, "Did it hurt?"

Maya answered only with a smile and he smiled back. He was glad Maya had the medicine in her arm.

By the time Kano had given the medicine to Grandmother, other women with their children were coming into the room. Grandmother showed them how to get their arms ready and Kano kept right on working.

When there were no more women or children waiting, Kano looked around and asked Grandmother, "Where is Maya?"

"She said she would be back soon and for us to wait for her."

"Grandmother, what can we do about the men in the Kashim?" Kano asked.

"The medicine man has said the women cannot take the men's food into the Kashim and wait there for the empty bowls. They must now wait at the door. This means I cannot go in to talk with the old men about you. And you cannot go into the Kashim unless they ask you to come in."

"Grandmother, this cannot wait. The men must be given the medicine. I am only a boy. If I go into the Kashim without being asked, all the men will be angry. If this happens, they will be against the medicine even more."

"Then I must go now to the Kashim," said Grandmother, "and if they will not listen to me, I will ask all the women of the village to go with me. The women fear for their men as they do for their children.

If I must, I will ask them to come into the Kashim with me and stay until the old men let you come in."

Grandmother was getting ready to go when they heard someone climbing down into the hallway. Both turned to look and saw first Maya and then the medicine man come from behind the caribou skin covering the doorway.

Kano could not speak. He had not once thought what would happen if the medicine man found out that he, Kano, was giving the white man's medicine to all the women and children in the village. Surely the medicine man should have been asked first, and now he would be angry.

Kano was even more surprised when he heard Maya say, "I have brought the medicine man here."

When she saw the look of surprise on Kano's face she quickly went on, "I have told him all that you have done. I have brought him here because I know he, too, wishes to help our people. And because I know he can help you by speaking to the men in the Kashim."

As soon as Maya stopped talking, the medicine man said, "Yes, I can help you, but we must go now. The sickness is already in our village and the men must have the medicine soon."

The medicine man's words told Kano he had nothing to fear so he asked, "And what would you have us do?"

"You, I, and your grandmother must go now to the Kashim, and you must bring the medicine with you," said the medicine man. "You will both go in with me. I will speak first to all the men there. I will ask your grandmother to speak for the women of the village. She will make the women's wishes known. She must also tell why the women took the medicine without first asking."

The three then left the house and entered the Kashim. Some of the men were still eating, but all stopped to listen as soon as they saw the medicine man.

Kano saw Napak sitting by the loved-fire and looking straight at him. Kano remembered what had happened in the Kashim last time and looked away.

Kano and Grandmother stood next to the medicine man as he spoke, "I have come to speak to all of you about the great sickness. Among the Eskimo many have died from it; and just this afternoon the yeg left the body of the one called 'Auntie' and she is no longer with us."

The medicine man stopped and a quiet murmur passed through the large room. Kano's heart was sad. He and the whole village would miss this woman who was never too busy to visit and listen to those who stopped by her house.

The medicine man went on, "This sickness travels quickly. It is new to our people and it is too strong for my medicine."

As he said these words a murmur again passed through the room. The medicine man stopped until it was quiet once more. "It is a sickness that the white man has brought and we must use the white man's medicine to fight it."

Now he stepped back and said, "I have asked the grandmother of Maya and Kano, the one called 'Basket-maker,' to speak for the women of our village."

Grandmother looked toward the old men as she said, "The women have asked Kano to give the medicine to all the women and children of our village and it is done. It gave the women great pain to do this without first asking the old men of the Kashim, for it is known that they are wise and that they spend much time thinking about what is good for our people. But the women feared for the lives of their children and so they did this."

Grandmother stopped and looked around at all the men before she added, "And now the women fear for the lives of their men and they ask that their men be given the medicine too."

Again the medicine man stepped forward. "Before, when the Russian came here to the Kashim, the old men had good reason not to let the medicine be given. They had heard the Eskimo tell how their people died after they took the white man's medicine. Now it is different. Many days ago Kano took the medicine and it has not made him sick."

He turned toward Kano as he spoke his next words, "It is Kano who learned from the Russian how to give the medicine and it is Kano who traveled across to the Innoko, all alone in yesterday's storm, to bring the medicine back to us. I believe he did not mean to go against the ways of our people when he took the medicine without asking first. I think he meant only to help and I ask the old men of the Kashim to remember this."

The medicine man turned now to where the old men sat as he said, "Now I ask you, the old men of this village, to think about all that has happened and all that has been said here and then tell us what you think should be done."

The old men spoke to each other but for a short time before the one called "Killer-of-bears" came forward and said, "We ask that all the men of the Kashim let Kano give them the medicine now."

Then Killer-of-bears looked at Kano and said, "By what he did yesterday, we believe Kano has shown that he wishes only to help his people. We think there is much we can take from the white man that will make the ways of our people better. Kano has shown us that the white man's medicine is one of those things. We welcome you, Kano, back to the Kashim. And when your father returns we shall tell him you have shown yourself to be a worthy son."

These words filled Kano's heart with happiness, but he was also glad when the medicine man came and asked him to make ready.

As Kano worked, Grandmother stood and showed each man how to make his arm ready. The medicine man stood in back of Kano and watched everything.

At last they were finished. All the men had taken the medicine, even Napak. Kano was glad.

While Kano was putting everything away, he heard the medicine man telling the men, "Some who have taken the medicine today might already have the sickness, even though they do not feel it. Because of this, days must pass before we can be sure the medicine will work for everyone. Go now to your homes and tell this to your wives."

The women waited and worried during those days and so did Kano. The fifth day passed and the sickness had come to only one other person. From what Ivan had told him, Kano felt sure the medicine had stopped the sickness. He told Maya and Grandmother about this and they in turn told the other women of the village.

That night, after talking to Maya, Kano left his house and went back to the Kashim to sleep. He stopped at the door of the Kashim and looked back. The wind blowing through the spruce trees on the hill in back of the village brought to his mind the night of his Feast of the First Hunt. How he had waited here at the door for Maya and the women to bring the meat from the moose he had killed.

Much had happened since that time. Soon his father would be back. Kano would ask him for one more chance to show that he could be a hunter for his people. Now he felt sure his fear would not keep him from doing what he must do.

And next year, before the Feast for the Dead to honor Auntie, he would hunt and bring meat to that feast for his people to eat.

Then, someday, he would go with his father to visit St. Michael. There, in the place of the white men, he could learn much to make the way of his people better. There, too, he might again meet his friend, Ivan.

# About the Author

Arnold Griese taught for several years in a one-room school in the Athabaskan village of Tanana in interior Alaska. At that time, traveling in his own plane to many other settlements along the Tanana, Yukon, and Koyukuk rivers, he came to know and love the Athabaskan people and to hear their tales of ancient days.

Mr. Griese grew up on a farm in Iowa, one of a large family to whom reading was always important. At seventeen he left the farm to find his fortune. His travels took him through most of the western states, and to Hawaii and Mexico. After service in World War II he was graduated from Georgetown University and earned his master's degree from the University of Miami and his doctorate at the University of Arizona. He went on to join the faculty of the University of Alaska as professor of children's literature.

Other titles by Arnold Griese include *Anna's Athabaskan Summer, The Wind Is Not a River* (A NCSS-CBC Notable Book), and *At the Mouth of the Luckiest River*, which *The New York Times* lauded as having "an aura of legend." He lives in Fairbanks, Alaska.